EYE TO EYE WITH HORSES

American Quarter Horses

Lynn M. Stone

Rourke

Publishing LLC

Vero Beach, Florida 32964

3 1257 01791 0711

www.rourkepublishing.com

PHOTO CREDITS: Title Page, pages 5, 10, 11, 12, 14 and 17 © Lynn M. Stone; pages 9, 15, 18, 20, 21 and 22 © American Quarter Horse Association; page 6 © Steven Robertson

Editor: Robert Stengard-Olliges

Cover and page design by Tara Raymo

Library of Congress Cataloging-in-Publication Data

Stone, Lynn M.
  American quarter horses / Lynn Stone.
    p. cm. -- (Eye to eye with horses)
  ISBN 978-1-60044-579-8
  1. Quarter horse--Juvenile literature. I. Title.
  SF293.Q3S76 2008
  636.1'33--dc22
                                        2007019098

Printed in the USA

CG/CG

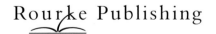

Rourke Publishing

www.rourkepublishing.com – rourke@rourkepublishing.com
Post Office Box 3328, Vero Beach, FL 32964

Table of Contents

Quarter Horses

The American Quarter Horse is the most popular horse **breed** in the United States. It is also the oldest of the all-American horse breeds.

Quarter Horses are perhaps the most **versatile** of horses. They serve many purposes. One of those purposes earned the Quarter Horse its name.

The versatile Quarter Horse is an all-American breed.

A Quarter Horse racing down the track.

The early English settlers of what would become the United States loved horse racing. By 1656 horse racing in the Virginia colony was popular. Over a one-quarter mile (.4 kilometer) distance, these horses could practically fly! The horses were raced through woods, on trails, and along village streets. The horses became known as "quarter-milers" or "quarter horses."

QUARTER HORSE FACTS

The American Quarter Horse Association (AQHA) formed in 1940. That is the year quarter horses were recognized as an official breed. But everyone knows the horses were around longer than that.

A **Thoroughbred** can beat a Quarter Horse in a one mile (1.6 km) race. But the Quarter Horse is still king of the quarter mile.

Quarter Horses bolt onto a California race track.

The History of American Quarter Horses

English settlers reached American shores in the 1600's. They found horses of the type brought to America by Spanish explorers in the 1500's. These horses were probably a mix of Spanish, Barb, and Arabian.

Spanish explorers brought a mix of horses to 16th century North America.

High quality Quarter Horses still depend upon selective breeding by their owners.

The settlers imported English "running horses." These were themselves a mix of breeds. To **cross** English and Spanish type horses, settlers picked parent horses carefully. That's called **selective breeding**. Eventually, their efforts resulted in a new breed – the American Quarter Horse. The Quarter Horse was stronger, faster, and more versatile than its ancestors.

Quarter Horses are loved for their ability to spring into a gallop.

The Quarter Horse has always been an animal of many abilities. It was far more than just a racing horse for the settlers. It was a farm horse. It was a cattle horse. It was a horse that could pull a carriage or a wagon. Fitted with a saddle, it was daily transportation for its rider. But perhaps most of all, settlers loved the Quarter Horse's ability to sprint at high speed from a standing start.

Thoroughbreds arrived in the United States in the 1700's. They raced on long oval tracks. Interest in Quarter Horse racing took a dive. Finally, Quarter Horse racing disappeared in the eastern states.

The arrival of Thoroughbred racing changed the role of the Quarter Horse in the east.

Pioneers brought the Quarter Horse west as a favorite "cow pony."

The Quarter Horse remained popular, though, especially in the West. The Quarter Horse was ideal for America's **migration** westward in the 1800's. After all, it was much more than just a running horse. It was tough and calm, and it was a good working and riding horse.

Quarter Horse racing is popular again. Races are held over 11 different distances. The longest is about one-half mile (805 meters).

Being a Quarter Horse

A Quarter Horse is compact and slightly chunky. It should have large, muscled hindquarters and a muscular neck. Hindquarter muscles give the quarter horse both speed and the ability to stop quickly.

A Quarter Horse stands from about 14.5 hands (58 inches, 149 centimeters) to just over 16 hands (64 inches, 164 centimeters) high. Its body is clearly shorter and wider than that of a Thoroughbred.

A Quarter Horse is compact, muscular, and agile.

Quarter Horses are often a shade of brown.

Quarter Horses come in many colors, some of which are bay, black, brown, buckskin, and palomino. Probably the most common coat is a reddish brown color known as sorrel. It may have a few white markings below its knees and on its face.

Owning a Quarter Horse

It's the all-American horse. Quarter Horse owners love it for its many abilities and its gentle nature. It's easily trained to the saddle and easily handled.

In cattle roping competition, a Quarter Horse shows off its great agility.

Quarter Horses are exceptional rodeo horses.

The Quarter Horse is a wonderful trail, or riding, horse. As a cow horse, it has speed, balance, and **agility**. It also has what cowboys call "cow sense." That's the Quarter Horse's remarkable **instinct** for rounding up cattle.

It's a fine rodeo horse, too. Quarter Horses are the choice for barrel racing, calf roping, and team roping events.

Up and over: A Quarter Horse competes in jumping shows too!

Glossary

agility (ah JIL uh tee) – being able to move easily and well; athletic

breed (BREED) – a group of domestic animals within a group (such as Quarter Horses), having the same basic characteristics

cross (KRAWSS) – to mate or match one breed with another breed

instinct (IN stingkt) – an inborn ability to know or do something

migration (MYE gray shuhn) – a distant journey

selective breeding (si LEK tiv bree DING) – the process of choosing an animal's parents

Thoroughbred (THUR oh bred) – a breed of horse developed in England for racing

versatile (VUR suh tuhl) – able to do many things well

Index

Further Reading

Dell, Pamela. *American Quarter Horses*. Child's World, 2007.
VanCleaf, Kristin. *Quarter Horses*. ABDO Publishing, 2006.

Website to Visit

www.aqha.com/
www.kyhorsepark.com/imh/bw/quar.html
www.ansi.okstate.edu/breeds/horses/quarter/

About the Author

Lynn M. Stone is the author of more than 400 children's books. He is a talented natural history photographer as well. Lynn, a former teacher, travels worldwide to photograph wildlife in its natural habitat.